Stephen F. Austin

The Father of Texas

Harriet Isecke, M.S.Ed. and
Stephanie Kuligowski, M.A.T.

Consultant

Devia Cearlock
K–12 Social Studies Specialist
Amarillo Independent School District

Publishing Credits

Dona Herweck Rice, *Editor-in-Chief*
Lee Aucoin, *Creative Director*
Marcus McArthur, Ph.D., *Associate Education Editor*
Neri Garcia, *Senior Designer*
Stephanie Reid, *Photo Editor*
Rachelle Cracchiolo, M.S.Ed., *Publisher*

Image Credits:
Cover State Preservation Board, Austin, Texas & Bridgeman Art Library; p.1 State Preservation Board, Austin, Texas; pp.1–2 Bridgeman Art Library; p.4 The Granger Collection; p.5 North Wind Picture Archives, (sidebar) Brazoria County Historical Museum; p.6 Tom Hogenmiller/Flickr; p.7, 8 North Wind Picture Archives; p.9 History Pictures; p.10 Corbis; p.11 (top) The Granger Collection, (bottom) University Of Texas; p.12 Alamy; p.13 State Preservation Board, Austin, Texas; p.14 Kameron K. Searle; p.15 The Granger Collection; p.16 (top) Newscom; p.16 (bottom) Jaontiveros/ Wikimedia; p.17 Perry–Castañeda Library Map Collection, University of Texas at Austin; p.18 Newscom; p.19 Newscom, (sidebar) Joseph–Siffred Duplessis [Public domain]; p.20 Alamy; p.21 The Granger Collection; p.22 (left) Newscom, (right) iStockphoto; p.23 Dolph Briscoe Center for American History, The University of Texas at Austin; p.25 Gonzales Memorial Museum; p.26 The Granger Collection ; p.27 Bridgeman Art Library; p.28 State Preservation Board, Austin, Texas; p.29 Angela Orlando/Flickr; All other images Shutterstock.

Teacher Created Materials
5301 Oceanus Drive
Huntington Beach, CA 92649-1030
http://www.tcmpub.com

ISBN 978-1-4333-5045-0

Printed by: 51497
Printed in: China

Table of Contents

The Young Austin

Future Entrepreneur

Stephen Fuller Austin was born into a family of **entrepreneurs** (ahn-truh-pruh-NOORZ). Entrepreneurs are bold risk takers who start new businesses. Austin took one of the biggest risks in American history. He started the first American **colony** in Texas.

Austin was the son of Moses and Mary Austin. He was born in Virginia on November 3, 1793. His father, who was nicknamed the Lead King, owned a lead mine.

Although the mine was successful, Moses was in debt. Soon, the mine failed. The Austin family moved west to make a new start. They headed for southeast Missouri, where lead was more plentiful.

Austin, Texas, 1840

Stephen F. Austin

Moses started another mining business. He founded the town of Potosi (puh-TOH-see), Missouri. The Austins were a wealthy and important family. They sent young Austin to boarding school. Moses told his son to study hard and work toward greatness. But he had no idea that his son would grow up to be known as the Father of Texas.

Moses Austin

Father of Industry

Moses Austin was an **innovative** businessman. Moses was not afraid to try new methods and test new ideas. He asked experts from England's lead mines for advice on updating his mines. His efforts started the lead industry in America.

The Austin Family

Moses and Mary Austin had five children, but only three survived to adulthood. Stephen Fuller was the oldest son. A daughter, Emily, was born in 1798. Another son, James Elijah (ih-LAHY-juh), was born in 1803.

Family Business

After finishing college, Austin returned to Missouri. He joined his father's mining business. He was also elected to Missouri's territorial legislature (LEJ-is-ley-cher). The legislature made laws for the area.

In 1819, America's first **economic depression** struck. It was called the *Panic of 1819*. To get the economy moving again, Austin's father helped start the Bank of St. Louis. He invested the family fortune in the bank. But the bank failed. The Austins lost almost everything.

Austin house in Missouri

Austin had planned to take over the family business. But now, there was no business. At age 27, he had to start over. Austin moved to Arkansas. He claimed land near present-day Little Rock.

In Arkansas, Austin held many different jobs. He ran for U.S. Congress but lost the election. He was chosen to be a local judge, but the job did not last long. When Little Rock was chosen to be the state capital, Austin hoped to **profit** from his land there. Instead, the court ruled that the land was not his to sell. Once again, Austin was derailed. But he was set on being successful.

Hard Times

The Panic of 1819 was the first major economic crisis in the United States. Europe started buying less American food than before. The U.S. government had borrowed too much money. Its banking system failed. But after four years, the economy improved.

Staking Claim

Austin had staked claim to land near present-day Little Rock, Arkansas. To claim a plot of land in those days, a person just had to live on it and make improvements to it. Austin did not realize that another person had also claimed the same land.

A New Colony

One Last Wish

In 1820, Austin moved to Louisiana. He studied to become a lawyer. At the same time, Austin's father, Moses, was trying to fix his money problems. He believed he could save the family fortune by starting an American colony in New Spain. New Spain was the territory south of the United States. It was owned by Spain, but very few Spanish people lived there. It was unsafe. The settlers had little protection from American Indian raids. So Spain invited Americans to help settle the territory.

map showing the territory of New Spain

In 1821, Moses traveled to Texas. He wanted permission to start a colony. The Spanish **postmaster**, Juan Erasmo Seguín (HOOWAHN eh-RAHS-mo seh-GEEN), gave him a **land grant**. Moses could bring 300 **Anglo** families to Texas. But on the trip home, Moses got sick. He died a few months later.

Austin was unsure about his father's plan for a Texas colony. But Moses's dying wish was for his son to take over the land grant. Austin could not deny his father's last wish.

Stephen F. Austin

Other Texas Colonists

There were many important Texas colonists before the Austins. José de Escandón (hoh-SAY deh ehs-kahn-DON) helped colonize South Texas. Damián Massanet (dah-mee-AHN mahs-sah-NET) founded the first Spanish mission in East Texas. And Martín De León (mahr-TEEN deh leh-OHN) was the only Mexican **empresario** (ehm-preh-SAH-ree-oh) to establish a colony in Texas.

A Son's Love

Austin loved his father very much. Austin wrote the following about his father's death: *"This news has affected me very much. He was one of the most feeling and affectionate Fathers that ever lived. His faults I now say, and always have, were not of the heart."*

Carrying On

Soon after his father's death, Austin set out for San Antonio. He needed permission to take over his father's land grant. He learned that Mexico had declared independence, or freedom, from Spain. Texas was no longer Spanish. It was now Mexican land.

Austin continued on his mission. The Spanish governor let Austin take over the land grant. Austin then explored the Gulf Coast. He wanted to find a good location for his colony. He chose the land between the Colorado and Brazos (BRAH-zohs) rivers.

Austin advertised the new colony across the country. Land there was priced at 12.5 cents per acre. With land in the rest of the country selling for $1.25 per acre, that was cheap!

Many people responded. But Austin chose his colonists carefully. He would be the police and the judge in the new colony. So he made people prove they were honest and hardworking.

Settlers sign up for Austin's Colony.

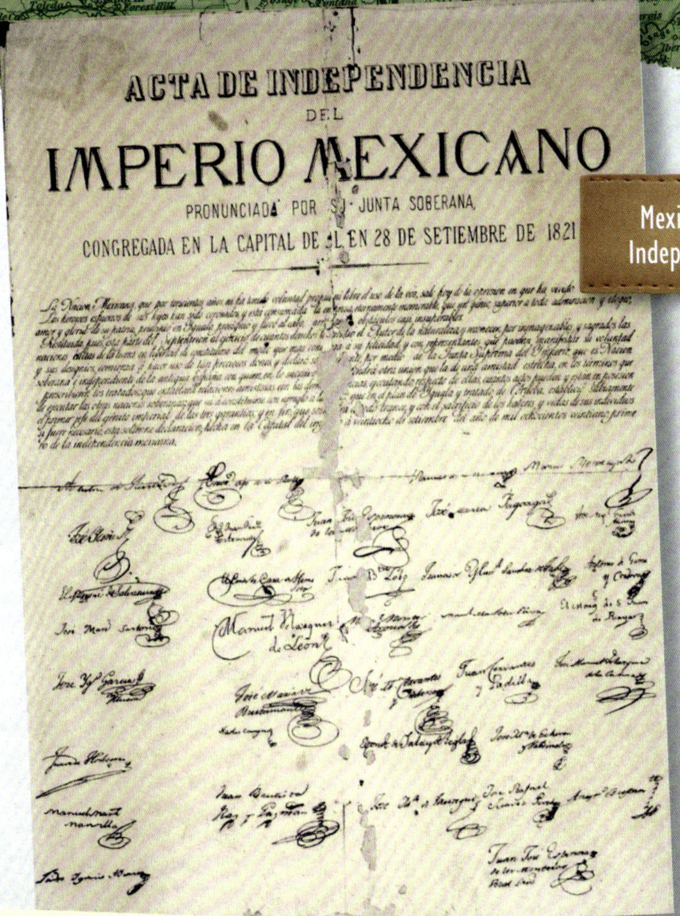
ACTA DE INDEPENDENCIA
DEL
IMPERIO MEXICANO
PRONUNCIADA POR SU JUNTA SOBERANA,
CONGREGADA EN LA CAPITAL DE EL EN 28 DE SETIEMBRE DE 1821

Mexico's Declaration of Independence from Spain

Real Estate Deals

The Spanish government set the amounts of land that Austin could give to settlers. A married man would get 640 acres of land, plus 320 acres for his wife. He also could claim an extra 320 acres for each child and 80 acres for each slave.

The Old 300

The first Anglo settlers to follow Austin to Texas are known as the Old 300. They moved to the land that was located between the Brazos and Colorado rivers. Most were successful businesspeople from the southern United States. American settlers living in Mexican Texas are known as **Texians**.

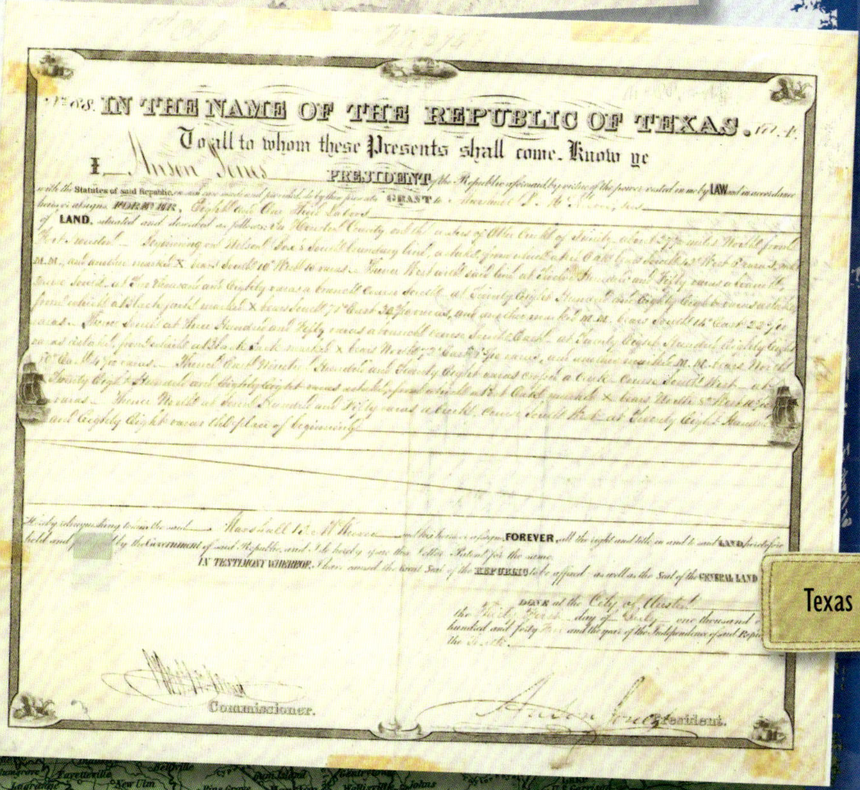
IN THE NAME OF THE REPUBLIC OF TEXAS.
To all to whom these Presents shall come. Know ye
PRESIDENT
LAND.
FOREVER
Commissioner.
President.

Texas land grant

Ranching and Farming

In 1823, Mexico passed the Imperial Colonization Law. This law encouraged people to settle in Texas. The law gave ranchers a **league**, or 4,428 acres, of grazing land. Farmers got a **labor**, or 177 acres, of farmland. Most people signed up as ranchers and farmers to get the maximum amount of land.

Rich in Real Estate

Austin earned 67,000 acres for every 200 families he brought to Texas. That is equal to 104 (269 km^2) square miles. Austin settled more than 1,000 colonists in Texas. By 1834, he had earned 197,000 acres of land for himself.

Moving to Mexico

The first Anglo settlers arrived in Texas in late 1821. But Austin had a problem. Mexico would not honor the Spanish land grant. Austin had to travel to Mexico City to make his case with the new government.

Austin's hand-drawn map of the province of Texas, around 1822

Austin prepares to fight American Indians in 1824.

Austin got Mexico to approve a new law. The law set up the empresario system. Under this system, men who started a colony and led settlers to Texas became empresarios. The more colonists a leader could bring, the more land he received.

In his dealings with Mexico, Austin had to make many promises. He promised that the colonists would follow Mexican rules. They would swear loyalty to Mexico's king. They would learn Spanish. And they would become Roman Catholic.

In 1824, Austin finally convinced Mexico to admit American colonists. Austin worked hard to help the colonists succeed in Texas. He even led them in fights against hostile American Indians. In turn, the colonists treated their leader with great respect.

Caught in the Middle

Austin wanted to keep the colonists happy. He also worked hard to keep peace with Mexico. But not all empresarios followed Austin's example. Haden Edwards was a wealthy farmer. He had a land grant to start a colony near Nacogdoches (nak-uh-DOH-chuhz), Texas. But some of the land had already been claimed. Edwards asked the current landowners to show proof of ownership. He said those who did not provide proof would have to give up their claims. Many colonists disliked this.

When the colony held its first mayoral election, Edwards lost. Many colonists complained about Edwards to Mexican leaders. Mexico took away Edwards's land contract. He was **expelled** from the country.

the Republic of Fredonia flag

Texas Rangers

Edwards was angry that he lost control of his own colony. He and his men put the mayor in jail. Then, they arrested the general of the local Mexican army.

Next, Edwards started a **rebellion**. He declared the colony's independence from Mexico. He called it the Republic of Fredonia (freh-DOH-nee-uh). He asked Austin to help him fight the Mexican Army. Austin refused. Instead, Austin helped the Mexican Army crush the rebellion.

The Texas Rangers

In August 1823, the Mexican government gave Austin permission to organize a group of 10 volunteers to protect his colony. The men would patrol the frontier and defend the settlers from attacks by American Indians. This new law enforcement agency became known as the Texas Rangers. They still exist as a law-enforcement agency in Texas.

Rebels Escape

Austin's men joined the Mexicans to end the Fredonian rebellion. But they never had to fight. By the time Austin's men got to Fredonia, Edwards and his men had fled to Louisiana.

Guadalupe Victoria

CONSTITUCION

FEDERAL

DE LOS ESTADOS UNIDOS MEXICANOS.

SANCIONADA

POR EL CONGRESO GENERAL CONSTITUYENTE,

EL 4 DE OCTUBRE DE

1824.

IMPRENTA DEL SUPREMO GOBIERNO DE LOS ESTADOS-UNIDOS MEXICANOS, EN PALACIO.

the Mexican Constitution of 1824

Law and Order

The colonists often faced American Indian attacks. They needed protection. But Mexico had very little money. It could not afford to protect everyone. So Mexico let colonists form **militias** (mi-LISH-uhs). Militias are armies of civilian soldiers.

Austin became head of his colony's militia. He had to keep law and order. In January 1824, he made the colony's laws. These were the first Anglo-American laws in Texas.

Also in 1824, Mexico wrote its first **constitution**, or set of laws. It made Mexico a **republic**. It had 19 states and four territories. The lands of Coahuila (kaw-ah-WEE-lah) and Tejas (TEY-has), or Texas, were combined. The new state was called *Coahuila y Tejas*.

The document was based on the U.S. Constitution. It set up three branches of government. They were the **executive**, the **legislative**, and the **judicial**. It also made Roman Catholicism the state religion.

Some of the new laws helped the Texian colonists. They were freed from their debts to the United States. The states also were allowed to make many of their own laws.

map of the Mexican Republic, 1824

First President

In 1824, Mexico became the United Mexican States. The first president was Guadalupe (gwad-uh-LOOP-eh) Victoria. He was an effective leader. He formed relations with many countries, including Great Britain, the United States, and the Federal Republic of Central America. Victoria also ended slavery in Mexico. In addition, he was a champion of education and culture.

Welcome to Mexico!

With the new constitution, the Mexican government relaxed its **immigration** rules. They welcomed American settlers to the Texas colonies. They hoped more settlers would provide protection from American Indian attacks.

Freemasons

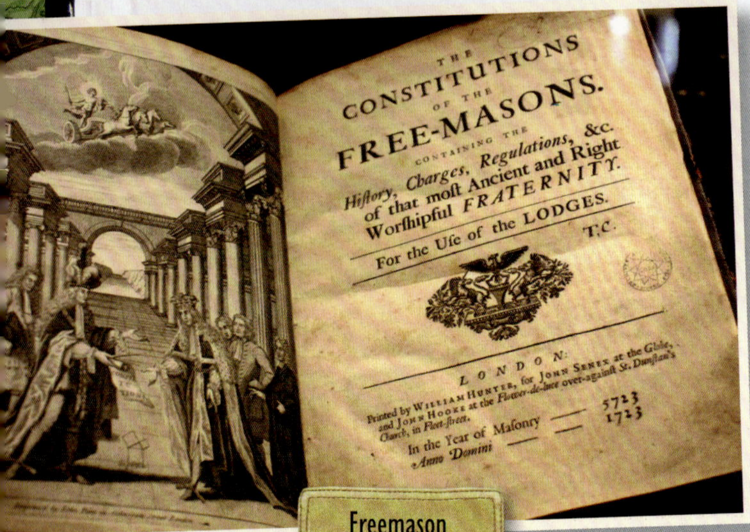
THE CONSTITUTIONS OF THE FREE-MASONS. CONTAINING THE Hiftory, Charges, Regulations, &c. of that moft Ancient and Right Worfhipful FRATERNITY. For the Ufe of the LODGES.

LONDON:

In the Year of Mafonry —— 5723

Anno Domini —— 1723

Freemason Constitutions

Before moving to Texas, Austin had joined the Freemasons. The Freemasons was a **fraternity**, or a social club. It claimed to promote friendship, brotherly love, and good conduct. The Freemasons were known for their secret **rituals** and symbols. Today, there are Freemasons in nearly every country.

In 1828, Austin decided to start a group of Freemasons in Texas. He knew there were Freemasons in Mexico City. He asked their permission to start a chapter in Texas. He waited a long time but never got a response.

Austin went ahead with his plans. He invited some of his friends to become Freemasons. The group met and elected officers. Austin was chosen as the chapter's leader.

Mexico worried about the Texas colonists starting a secret society. Some feared that Freemasons would try to make Texas a free country. Others felt the group went against Church teachings. Soon, Mexico outlawed the Freemasons in Texas.

Austin respected Mexico and obeyed the new law. He announced that the group would no longer meet. This made some people angry. They thought Austin should have stood up to Mexican leaders.

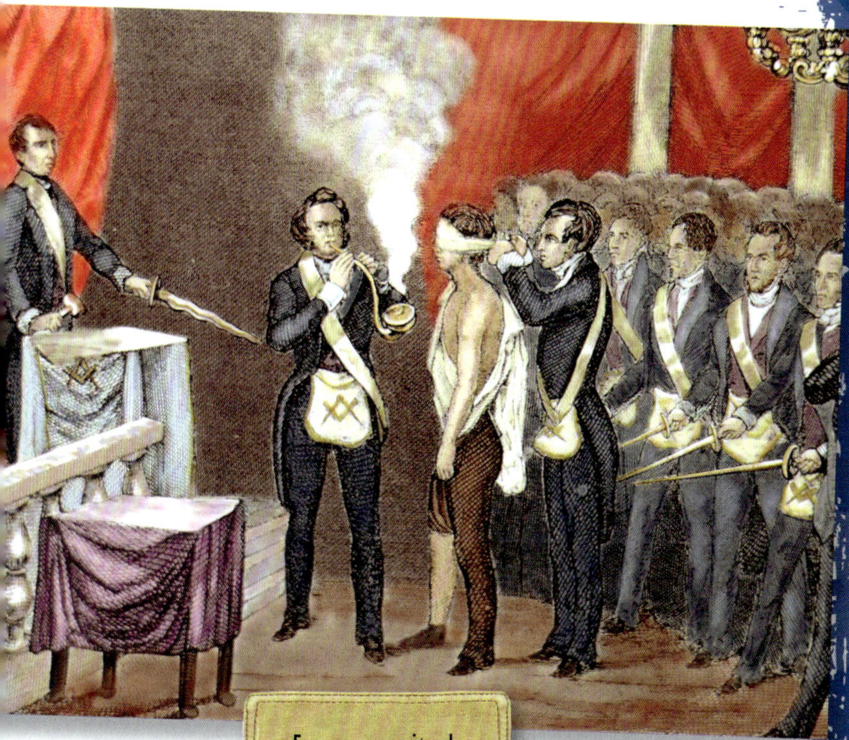

Freemason ritual

Benjamin Franklin

In Good Company

Throughout history, many famous men have been Freemasons. That list includes important figures in American history, such as Paul Revere, Benjamin Franklin, and George Washington. Fourteen U. S. presidents have been Freemasons.

Many Critics

Freemasons have always had their share of critics. Some Americans were suspicious of the group. They wondered if Freemasons were so secretive because they had something bad to hide. Religious groups, such as the Roman Catholic Church, were their most vocal **opponents**. These religious groups felt that Freemason beliefs went against the teachings of Christianity.

Tensions Rise

Slavery in Texas

By 1830, American colonists were pouring into Texas. Most of them were from the American South. The Mexicans worried that Americans were taking over Texas.

Some of the colonists brought their slaves with them. Slavery was illegal in Mexico. But Austin's empresario contract allowed it in Texas. Austin did not like slavery. But he knew that some Southerners would not move to Texas without their slaves. Of the 1,800 colonists in Austin's Colony in 1825, 443 were slaves.

For a decade, the Mexican government threatened to free the slaves in Texas. Finally, the Law of April 6, 1830, banned slavery in Texas. It increased Mexican control of Texas. It also banned Americans from moving to Texas.

slaves picking cotton

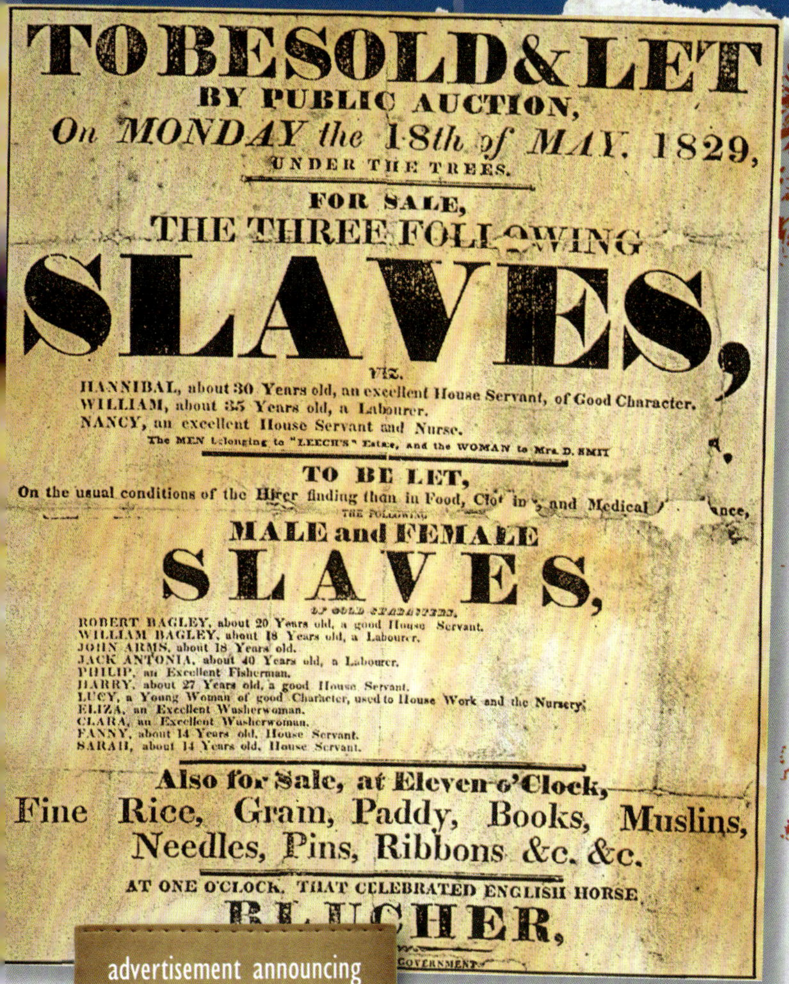

advertisement announcing sale of slaves

The Law of April 6, 1830, angered many Texans. Many believed they needed slaves to farm their huge plots of land. They did not want to pay their workers. Their solution was to form the independent state of Texas. At the Convention of 1833, Texans wrote a constitution for their proposed state.

Adding Fuel to the Fire

Mexican general Manuel de Mier y Terán (mee-YEHR ee teh-RAHN) sent Juan Davis Bradburn to the Texas town of Anahuac (uh-NAH-wahk). He was to enforce the Law of April 6, 1830. He collected taxes and made sure no new settlers got land. The Texans did not like Bradburn.

Bradburn further angered Texans when he refused to send two runaway slaves back to their master. Then, he unjustly arrested two Texans.

The Texans fought back. In June 1832, around 200 Texans marched to Anahuac. They captured 19 of Bradburn's men and took control of the town. These events are known as the Anahuac Disturbances.

Austin Is Arrested

The Convention of 1833 chose Austin to bring the new Texas constitution to Mexican leaders. Austin arrived in Mexico City in July 1833.

Austin spent several months in Mexico City pushing for changes in Texas. He convinced the government to **repeal** the Law of April 6, 1830. But Mexican president Antonio López de Santa Anna (ahn-TOH-nee-oh LOH-pehs deh SAHN-tah AH-nah) refused to make Texas a state. He wanted to control Texas. He did not want to give American colonists more freedom.

In December 1833, Austin headed home. Before he got home, he was arrested for trying to start a rebellion. Mexican officials took him to prison in Mexico City.

Antonio López de Santa Anna

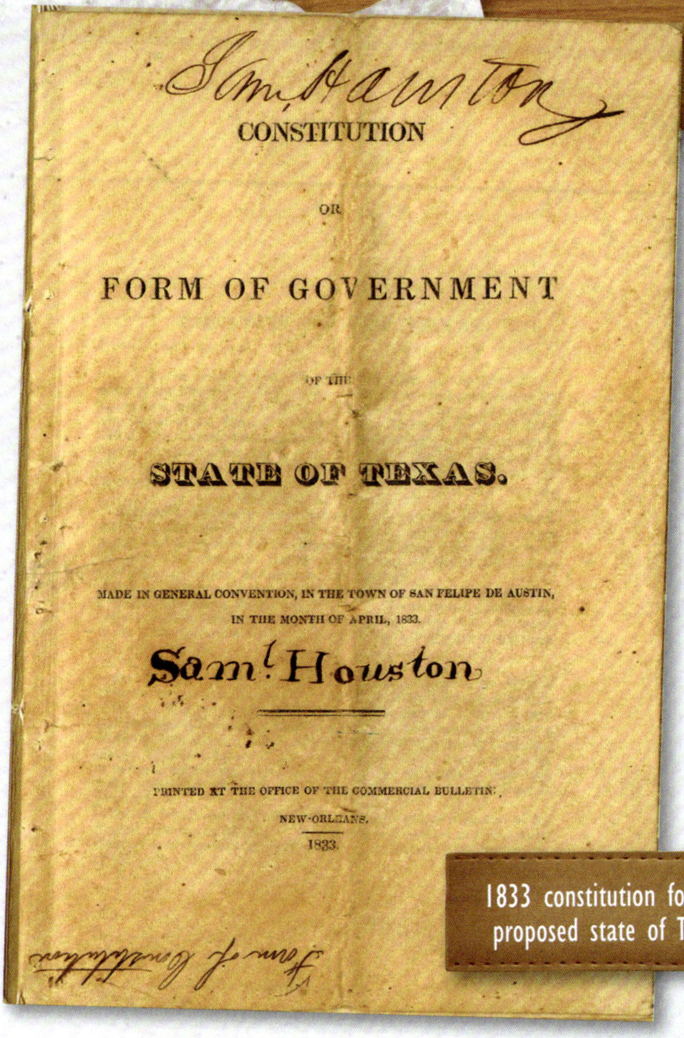
CONSTITUTION

OR

FORM OF GOVERNMENT

OF THE

STATE OF TEXAS.

MADE IN GENERAL CONVENTION, IN THE TOWN OF SAN FELIPE DE AUSTIN, IN THE MONTH OF APRIL, 1833.

Saml Houston

PRINTED AT THE OFFICE OF THE COMMERCIAL BULLETIN: NEW-ORLEANS. 1833.

1833 constitution for the proposed state of Texas

No charges were filed against Austin. His case never went to trial. He was released the next year. But he was not allowed to leave the city. Finally, in early 1835, Austin was free to return to Texas.

Austin had always been able to solve conflicts between the Texas and Mexico. But he knew he could not keep the peace forever. Austin began to support Texas independence.

Stephen F. Austin

Peacemaker

Austin had long played the role of peacemaker between American settlers and the Mexican government. But in the 1830s, this became even more difficult.

The Mexican government wanted to increase its control of Texas. The American settlers wanted more freedom. Austin was finally forced to choose sides. He no longer saw a future for Anglo Texas as part of Mexico. He now called for war against Mexico. He wanted Texas to be independent.

the flag that women at Gonzales made to fly over the cannon

The Texas Revolution

The First Shots

Mexican president Santa Anna wanted to strengthen the Mexican government. He also wanted to take power away from the states. Texans did not like this. Santa Anna was taking away their freedoms.

Santa Anna heard about the Mexican loss at Anahuac. He was convinced that the colonists had to go. He planned to rid Texas of all American colonists. But first, he ordered his army to **disarm** their militias.

Mexico had given the Texas settlers in Gonzales a cannon to use against American Indians. Now, the Mexican Army ordered the Texans to return it. The Texans refused.

More than 100 Mexican soldiers went to Gonzales to take the cannon. High water in the Guadalupe River stopped them. On the other side of the river, 18 Texans stood ready to fight.

On the morning of October 2, 1835, Texan volunteers at Gonzales attacked the Mexicans. A Mexican officer again ordered the Texans to return the cannon. But the Texans pointed to the cannon behind them and said, "Come and take it!" The Texans won the Battle of Gonzales. The Texas **Revolution** had begun.

the cannon that fired the first shot of the Texas Revolution

Not Alone

Other Mexican states were angry that Santa Anna wanted to take away their freedoms, too. Like Texas, two other states declared their independence from Mexico. For a short time, there was a Republic of Yucatán (yoo-kuh-TAN) and a Republic of the Rio Grande.

Forming an Army

The army of Texan volunteers defeated the Mexicans at the Battle of Gonzales. But the Texans knew they needed a real army to win a war for independence. They chose Austin to lead the Texian Army.

Fierce Fighting

Austin led the new Texian (TEK-see-uhn) Army to present-day San Antonio. There they won another battle. Texian and **Tejano** (tay-HA-no) volunteers moved into an old mission called *the Alamo* in December 1835. Austin was sent to New Orleans, where he served as the Texas **commissioner**, or agent, to the United States.

the Battle of the Alamo, 1836

General Santa Anna and his troops surprised the Texans by arriving in San Antonio on February 23, 1836. The Mexican Army attacked the Alamo. Around 150 Texians and Tejanos bravely defended the Alamo for 13 days.

On March 6, Mexican troops stormed the Alamo. They climbed the walls and blasted open the doors. The Texians and Tejanos fought to their deaths. Santa Anna killed all the survivors.

the Goliad Massacre

Just a few weeks later, the Texian Army was ready to take revenge on Santa Anna's troops. In the Battle of San Jacinto (sahn ha-SEEN-toh), the Texians took the Mexican troops by surprise. The Texians defeated them in just 18 minutes. About 630 of the Mexican soldiers were killed and 730 were captured. Only nine Texians died.

Santa Anna was captured the next day and was forced to sign a peace treaty. Texas had won its independence!

"Remember Goliad"

In March 1836, Mexican and Texian troops clashed in several battles near Goliad (GO-lee-ad). The Mexican Army defeated the Texians and marched survivors to Goliad. They were put in prison. Santa Anna ordered for them to be killed.

On March 27, about 400 Texian soldiers were killed in what became known as the Goliad **Massacre**. This event was a great motivator for the Texian volunteers. They wanted to avenge their fallen neighbors. As they stormed the Mexican Army at San Jacinto, they shouted, "Remember Goliad!"

The Father of Texas

Austin was still in New Orleans when he heard that Texas had won its independence from Mexico. He rushed back to Texas.

Austin was unsure if he wanted to be president of Texas. But he decided that he would serve if Texans chose him. Two weeks before the election, Sam Houston decided to run for Texas president, too.

Houston was a war hero. He had led the Texian Army in their final victory of the Texas Revolution. When the votes were counted, Houston had 10 times more votes than Austin. Austin became Texas's secretary of state. He was responsible for helping Texas get along with other governments. Given his history of making peace, this was the perfect job for Austin.

Stephen F. Austin

statue honoring Austin near Angleton, Texas

In December, Austin was at work in the new Texas Capitol Building. He was sick with what seemed to be a cold. But it turned out to be **pneumonia** (noo-MOHN-yuh). Doctors were called, but it was too late. Austin died on December 27, 1836.

When Houston heard about Austin's death, he said, "The Father of Texas is no more. The first pioneer of the wilderness has departed."

Counting Votes

Three men ran for President of the new Republic of Texas in 1836. They were Stephen F. Austin, Samuel Houston, and Henry Smith. Houston got most of the soldiers' votes. He ended up with 5,119 votes. Henry Smith got 743 votes, and Austin got 587 votes.

Living Legacy

Austin's importance to Texas history can be seen by the institutions that bear his name today. Since his death, there have been two colleges, a city, and a county named after Austin. Several monuments have also been created to honor Austin's legacy in the history of Texas.

Glossary

Anglo—a white person of European descent

colony—a country or area under the control of another country; a group of people living there

commissioner—an agent or person representing an organization

constitution—a written statement outlining the basic laws for a state or country

disarm—to take someone's weapons

economic depression—a period in which an economy is affected by unemployment, low output, and poverty

empresario—a person given a land grant by the Mexican government to make a settlement and recruit people to live there

entrepreneurs—people who start their own businesses

executive—the branch of government responsible for carrying out the laws

expelled—to be permanently kicked out

fraternity—a social club for men

immigration—the act of moving to a new country

innovative—doing new things or things in new ways

judicial—the branch of government responsible for enforcing the laws

labor—a plot of land measuring 177 acres, issued for planting crops

land grant—a contract that gives ownership of a plot of land

league—a plot of land measuring 4,428 acres, issued for grazing livestock

legislative—the branch of government responsible for making laws

massacre—a killing of many people

militias—groups of citizen soldiers

opponents—people who are against other people

pneumonia—a serious lung infection that makes it hard to breathe

postmaster—a person in charge of a post office

profit—to make money in business

rebellion—open resistance to one's government

repeal—to officially undo a law

republic—a political system in which people elect representatives to make laws for them

revolution—an act of overthrowing and replacing one government with another

rituals—acts or actions performed for a ceremony

Tejano—a Mexican-born Texan

Texians—people living in Mexican Texas between 1821 and 1836

Index

Your Turn!

Stephen F. Austin led the first Anglo settlers to Texas in 1821. He worked hard to make the colony a success. To protect the colonists from raids by hostile American Indians, he organized a group of 10 volunteers. The men patrolled the frontier and defended the colony. This new law enforcement agency became known as the Texas Rangers.

Austin's Top 10

The Texas Rangers were one of Stephen Austin's great ideas. Make a top-10 list of Austin's best ideas. Support the items on your list with facts from the text.